101 CREATIVE THINGS TO DO IN RETIREMENT

Retired but NOT Tired of Life and Adventure!

A List of Budget Leisure Ideas for Men and Women for the time when You Don't Need to Work Anymore!

Clarissa Lane

© Copyright 2025. All Rights Reserved

All rights reserved. No part of this book may be reproduced, distributed, or transmitted in any form or by any means, including photocopying, recording, or other electronic or mechanical methods, without the prior written permission of the publisher, except in the case of brief quotations embodied in critical reviews and certain other noncommercial uses permitted by copyright law.

Disclaimer Notice:

The information provided in this book is intended for general informational purposes only. The author and publisher make no representations or warranties regarding the accuracy, completeness, or suitability of the content for any particular purpose. Readers are encouraged to seek professional advice and perform their own due diligence before making any decisions based on the information contained herein. The author and publisher shall not be held responsible for any loss, injury, or damage resulting from the use of or reliance on the information provided.

"Aging is not 'lost youth' but a new stage of opportunity and strength."

— Betty Friedan

Table of Contents

Introduction 7

Family and Friends 9

Self-Growth 18

Hobbies and Crafts 31

Travel and Adventure 52

Physical Activities 70

Style and Image Updates 83

Digital World 89

Volunteering 96

Creative Expressions 101

Hodgepodge 107

Introduction

Retirement marks the beginning of a new phase in life, full of opportunities for personal growth and exploration. It's a time to pursue interests and passions that may have been set aside during your working years. Engaging in new activities can bring joy, fulfillment, and a renewed sense of purpose. Importantly, these pursuits don't always require significant financial investment.

Embracing New Opportunities: Retirement provides the freedom to explore new avenues and experiences. It's a time to redefine yourself, discover hidden talents, and expand your horizons. Whether it's picking up a new hobby, traveling to new places, or learning new skills, the possibilities are endless. This period can be one of the most enriching chapters of your life.

Financial Considerations: While some hobbies and activities can be expensive, retirement doesn't have to be a costly affair. There are countless ways to stay engaged and fulfilled without spending a lot of money. Many enriching activities are affordable or even free, ensuring that everyone can enjoy a rewarding retirement regardless of their financial situation.

The next chapter will explore 101 ideas for activities and pursuits that can enrich your life in retirement. These ideas will cover a range of interests and budgets, ensuring that there is something for everyone to enjoy.

Family and Friends

Mend Fences

Reach Out First: Take the initiative to contact the person you've had a conflict with. A simple message or call to express your desire to reconcile can open the door to healing. It's not about who's right or wrong but about restoring a positive connection.

Acknowledge and Apologize: Admit your part in the disagreement and offer a sincere apology. Acknowledging the other person's feelings can go a long way in rebuilding trust. Focus on the future rather than dwelling on past mistakes.

Listen Actively: Give the other person space to share their perspective. Listen without interrupting and show empathy for their feelings. Understanding their viewpoint can help you both move forward with mutual respect.

Set New Boundaries: After discussing the issues, establish clear boundaries to prevent similar conflicts in the future. Agree on how to communicate and resolve differences respectfully. This will strengthen your relationship and help maintain peace.

Family Karaoke

Create Lasting Memories: Family karaoke nights offer a unique opportunity to bond with loved ones in a fun and relaxed setting. By singing together, family members can share laughter, celebrate each other's talents, and create cherished memories that will last a lifetime.

Encourage Creativity and Confidence: Karaoke encourages everyone to step out of their comfort zone and showcase their singing abilities. It's a great way for people of all ages to express themselves creatively and build self-confidence while having a great time.

Strengthen Family Connections: Regular karaoke sessions help strengthen family ties by providing a regular activity that brings everyone together. It's an inclusive activity that allows each member to participate, fostering closer relationships and improving communication.

Versatile Entertainment: Karaoke is adaptable for any occasion. You can tailor the song choices and themes to match the event, making it a versatile entertainment option that keeps everyone engaged and entertained.

Reconnecting with School Friends

Revive Old Friendships: Reach out to classmates you haven't seen in years. Use social media or alumni networks to locate old friends and start conversations. Reconnecting can be a heartwarming experience, rekindling memories and strengthening old bonds.

Organize Reunions: Plan casual gatherings or virtual meet-ups with former classmates. These events provide opportunities to catch up, share life stories, and celebrate shared experiences. Reunions can be simple, from a coffee meetup to a full-blown party, depending on the group's preferences.

Share Memories: Exchange old photos and memorabilia with your friends. Reminiscing about past events, school projects, and fun moments can foster a deeper connection and provide a sense of nostalgia and continuity.

Create New Experiences: Take the opportunity to explore new activities together. Whether it's a book club, hobby group, or local event, creating new memories with old friends can strengthen your renewed friendship and bring a fresh perspective to your shared history.

Family Hiking Escapades

Quality Time Together: Family hikes are a wonderful way to bond with loved ones, away from the usual daily routines. Enjoying nature together helps strengthen family ties and creates cherished memories.

Health Benefits: Hiking is a beneficial physical activity that supports cardiovascular health, boosts mood, and enhances overall fitness. It's a fun way for the entire family to stay active and healthy.

Exploring New Trails: Each hike offers the chance to discover new trails and scenic views, adding an element of excitement to your outdoor adventures. Exploring different routes keeps the experience fresh and engaging.

Learning and Connecting with Nature: Hiking provides opportunities to learn about local wildlife and plants, fostering a deeper appreciation for nature. It's an enriching experience that enhances your connection to the natural world.

New Friendships

Be Open and Approachable: When meeting new people, be open to conversations and show genuine interest in others. Building friendships often starts with small talk and a willingness to engage. Being approachable and friendly makes it easier for others to connect with you.

Explore Local Activities: Engage in community events, clubs, or classes that interest you. Whether it's joining a book club, attending local workshops, or participating in hobby groups, these activities provide opportunities to meet people with similar interests.

Volunteer: Volunteering is a great way to connect with others who share your values. By contributing your time to causes you care about, you can build meaningful relationships while making a positive impact in your community.

Join Social Groups: Look for social organizations or support groups in your area. Many communities have groups specifically for socializing, networking, or special interests. These settings are conducive to forming new friendships and expanding your social circle.

Family Keepsakes

Gather Materials: Start by collecting a variety of family photos, letters, and documents. Look for images from different family events, milestones, and candid moments. Include letters, postcards, and mementos that tell a story or hold sentimental value.

Organize and Sort: Arrange the materials chronologically or by themes such as holidays, special occasions, or family traditions. This will help create a coherent narrative. Consider using photo-safe albums or digital tools for organization.

Add Personal Touches: Enhance the album with personal stories, anecdotes, and reflections. Include handwritten notes or printed captions that provide context or share memories related to the photos. This adds depth and personalization to the album.

Create and Preserve: Assemble the album by adhering photos and documents securely. For a digital album, use editing software to add captions and organize content. Make copies for family members or consider creating a digital version to share easily.

Tracing Family Roots

Discover Your Ancestry: Delving into your family's past can be a rewarding journey. By exploring genealogy, you gain a deeper understanding of where you come from, uncovering stories that have shaped your family's history.

Getting Started: Begin by gathering basic information from family members. Ask about relatives, birthplaces, and significant family events. This firsthand knowledge forms the foundation for your research.

Expand Your Search: Utilize online resources like ancestry databases, public records, and historical documents to trace your lineage further. Libraries and local archives can also be valuable sources of information.

Preserve and Share: As you build your family tree, consider documenting your findings in a format that can be shared with future generations. A well-documented history not only preserves your legacy but also connects family members to their shared heritage.

Time Capsule

Choose Meaningful Items: Select items that represent your current life and values. These could include photographs, letters, small keepsakes, newspaper clippings, or a favorite recipe. Consider including a few predictions or goals for the future.

Pick a Location: Decide on a special location to bury or store the time capsule. It could be your backyard, a favorite park, or a spot with sentimental value. Ensure the location is memorable and safe from potential damage.

Write a Letter: Include a letter to the future, expressing your hopes, dreams, and reflections on the present. This letter will be a heartfelt message to yourself or future generations when the capsule is eventually opened.

Seal and Mark: Carefully seal the capsule to protect its contents from the elements. Mark the location with a subtle yet memorable indicator, such as a small engraved stone or a detailed map, ensuring it can be easily found when the time comes to unearth it.

Self-Growth

Mastering the Art of Saying 'No'

The Power of Boundaries: Learning to say 'No' is essential for maintaining personal boundaries. It allows you to protect your time, energy, and well-being, ensuring that you focus on what truly matters to you. This skill helps prevent burnout and keeps your priorities in check.

Overcoming Guilt: Many people struggle with saying 'No' due to feelings of guilt or obligation. Understanding that it's okay to prioritize your needs is the first step toward overcoming these emotions. It's about realizing that saying 'No' doesn't make you selfish, but rather self-aware.

Practical Techniques: Start by practicing in low-stakes situations, such as declining small requests. Use phrases like 'I can't commit to this right now' or 'I'm unable to help with that.' As you build confidence, you'll find it easier to assert yourself in more significant scenarios.

Long-term Benefits: Mastering the art of saying 'No' leads to a more balanced and fulfilling life. It empowers you to invest your time and energy into activities and relationships that align with your values, ultimately leading to greater satisfaction and peace of mind.

Drone Skills

Practical Uses: Mastering drone piloting allows for capturing stunning aerial photos and videos, ideal for personal projects or professional use in real estate and agriculture. Drones are also useful for monitoring environments and assisting in search and rescue missions.

Learning Resources: Start with online courses or local workshops that teach drone operation and safety. Joining a drone club can also offer hands-on experience and guidance from experienced pilots.

Regulations and Safety: Learn about local drone regulations, including no-fly zones and required permits. Ensure safety by practicing in open areas and following best practices to prevent accidents.

Community Engagement: Connect with online forums or local groups of drone enthusiasts. These communities provide support, advice, and opportunities to enhance your skills through meetups and competitions.

The Art of Negotiation

Enhanced Communication: Effective negotiation improves communication skills, helping you articulate needs and understand others better. This can lead to more productive and harmonious interactions in both personal and professional settings.

Conflict Resolution: Mastering negotiation helps resolve conflicts amicably. By learning to find common ground and propose win-win solutions, you can handle disagreements more effectively and maintain positive relationships.

Opportunities for Growth: Negotiation skills open doors to new opportunities, whether it's securing better deals, advancing in volunteer roles, or navigating social situations. Being adept at negotiation increases your ability to influence outcomes in your favor.

Learning Resources: Numerous resources are available to learn negotiation skills. Consider enrolling in online courses, attending workshops, or reading books on negotiation techniques. Practicing with friends or in low-stakes situations can also build confidence and competence.

Self-Defense Skills

Enhanced Safety: Knowing self defense techniques can help protect against potential threats and increase personal security. It provides the skills to respond effectively in various situations, giving peace of mind.

Boosted Confidence: Mastering self-defense can enhance self-esteem and reduce fear. It builds a sense of control and preparedness, which can positively impact daily life and interactions.

Accessible Training: Self-defense classes are available at local community centers, gyms, and martial arts schools. Many organizations offer beginner-friendly courses designed to fit different skill levels and schedules. Online tutorials and virtual classes can also be valuable resources.

Physical and Mental Benefits: Engaging in self-defense training promotes physical fitness and mental sharpness. It involves exercise, strategic thinking, and stress relief, contributing to overall well-being.

New Language Skills

Boosts Memory: Engaging with a new language stimulates brain function and improves memory. The mental exercise involved in learning vocabulary, grammar, and pronunciation enhances cognitive abilities and keeps the mind sharp.

Enhances Cognitive Function: Language learning improves problem-solving skills and enhances overall mental flexibility. It challenges the brain to think in different ways, which can delay cognitive decline and contribute to better mental health.

Cultural Connection: Acquiring a new language opens doors to understanding and appreciating different cultures. This can lead to meaningful interactions with people from diverse backgrounds and enrich one's social life.

Effective Learning: To learn a new language effectively, consider online courses, language exchange programs, and immersive experiences. Apps and software offer flexibility, while joining local language groups or classes provides structured learning and practice opportunities.

Mindful Practice

Health Benefits: Regular meditation reduces stress, anxiety, and depression. It also lowers blood pressure and enhances emotional stability and concentration. Long-term practice can contribute to better overall health.

Getting Started: Explore basic meditation techniques like mindfulness or guided meditation. Online resources, such as apps and instructional videos, are great for beginners. Local classes or community centers may also offer in-person guidance.

Building a Routine: Start with short sessions, even just a few minutes a day, and gradually increase as you become more comfortable. Creating a consistent practice time and a tranquil space can enhance the effectiveness of your meditation.

Finding Support: Joining a meditation group or community can offer valuable support and encouragement. Connecting with others who meditate can provide motivation, resources, and insights to deepen your practice.

Mastering Public Speaking

Boosts Confidence: Learning to speak in public enhances self-assurance and helps overcome fears. It encourages effective communication and helps in various social and professional situations.

Improves Communication Skills: Mastering public speaking improves overall communication abilities, including clarity, persuasion, and engagement. This can lead to more successful interactions in both personal and professional settings.

Expands Opportunities: Being skilled in public speaking can lead to new opportunities, such as leading workshops, participating in community events, or even pursuing roles that require strong communication skills.

Accessible Learning Resources: There are numerous ways to learn public speaking. Online courses, local workshops, and public speaking clubs like Toastmasters provide practical training and feedback. Practicing regularly and seeking constructive criticism can significantly enhance your speaking abilities.

Silent Communication

Enhanced Communication Skills: Mastering sign language opens up a new way to communicate, bridging gaps with the Deaf and hard-of-hearing communities. It fosters inclusivity and improves interpersonal skills by adding another layer of expression.

Cognitive Benefits: Learning a new language, including sign language, stimulates cognitive functions, enhances memory, and sharpens problem-solving abilities. It can keep the mind active and engaged.

Learning Resources: There are various ways to learn sign language. Online courses, local classes, and community workshops provide accessible options. Many resources also include practice with native sign language users, which can be invaluable for mastering the language.

Community Connection: Engaging with the Deaf community through sign language can be deeply rewarding. It offers opportunities for social interaction, volunteering, and connecting with others who share an interest in communication and inclusivity.

Digital Literacy

Understanding Digital Literacy: Digital literacy is the ability to navigate, evaluate, and create information using digital technologies. It encompasses a range of skills from basic computer use to understanding how to stay safe online and utilize various digital tools.

Why It Matters: In today's world, being digitally literate is crucial. It allows you to stay connected with loved ones, manage your finances, access information, and participate in social and community activities. It also opens up new opportunities for learning and personal growth.

Learning Digital Skills: There are numerous resources available to help you improve your digital literacy. Online courses, local workshops, and community centers often provide training on how to use computers, smartphones, and the internet effectively. Practice regularly to build confidence.

Staying Safe Online: As you learn to navigate the digital world, it's important to understand online safety. This includes recognizing potential threats like phishing scams, protecting your personal information, and using secure passwords. Staying informed and cautious ensures a positive online experience.

First Aid Training

Lifesaving Skills: Learning first aid equips you with essential skills that can make the difference between life and death in emergencies. Whether it's CPR, wound care, or handling fractures, this knowledge ensures you're prepared to respond effectively.

Confidence in Crisis: First aid training boosts your confidence to take control in stressful situations. Knowing what to do during an emergency reduces panic and increases the chances of a positive outcome.

Community Contribution: With first aid skills, you can assist not just your family, but also neighbors and strangers in need. This ability to help others fosters a sense of community and strengthens bonds.

Accessible Learning: First aid courses are widely available online and in person. Many organizations, like the Red Cross, offer certified programs that can be completed in a few hours. Regular refreshers ensure your skills remain sharp.

Wilderness Survival Skills

Essential Life Skill: Learning survival skills in the wilderness equips you with the knowledge to handle unexpected situations. From finding water to building a shelter, these skills can be lifesaving and empowering, giving you confidence in any environment.

Connection with Nature: This skill set deepens your understanding and appreciation of nature. It allows you to experience the natural world in its purest form, fostering a sense of harmony and respect for the environment.

Learning and Training: You can acquire these skills through workshops, courses, or guided wilderness expeditions. Many organizations offer hands-on training that covers everything from basic first aid to advanced survival techniques.

Practical Applications: Beyond emergencies, these skills can be used in outdoor activities such as hiking, camping, and exploring remote areas. They also provide a unique opportunity to challenge yourself and grow mentally and physically, making every adventure more rewarding.

Breaking Bad Habits

Identify the Habits: Recognize which habits are problematic. Common ones include procrastination, excessive smoking or drinking, poor eating habits, and negative thinking. Acknowledging these habits is the first step toward change.

Understand the Impact: Consider how these habits affect your health, relationships, and overall quality of life. For example, smoking can lead to serious health issues, while procrastination can result in increased stress and missed opportunities.

Develop a Plan: Create a structured approach to overcome these habits. This might involve setting clear goals, finding healthier alternatives, and seeking support from friends, family, or professionals. Breaking a habit often requires gradual change and persistence.

Reap the Benefits: By addressing and overcoming bad habits, you can improve your health, boost your self-esteem, and enhance your overall well-being. The process might be challenging, but the positive changes are well worth the effort.

Hobbies and Crafts

Exotic Gardening

Choosing Plants: Start with tropical and subtropical plants that thrive indoors or in warm climates. Popular choices include orchids, bromeliads, and passionflowers. Research each plant's specific needs to ensure successful growth.

Optimal Conditions: Many exotic plants require specific conditions such as high humidity and warm temperatures. Use grow lights if natural light is insufficient and consider humidifiers to maintain moisture levels.

Growing Space: Depending on your climate, you might need a greenhouse or a sunroom to grow these plants. For those in cooler regions, indoor gardening with appropriate lighting and humidity control is essential.

Care and Maintenance: Regular watering, proper fertilization, and pest management are crucial. Follow guidelines specific to each plant, and keep an eye out for common issues such as fungal infections or pests.

The Art of Origami

Basics of Origami: Origami involves folding paper into various shapes and figures without the use of scissors or glue. The simplicity of the materials combined with the complexity of the designs makes it a fascinating craft.

Getting Started: Begin with a few basic folds and simple projects, such as cranes or boats. Use square paper and follow beginner-friendly instructions available in books or online tutorials. Practice is key to mastering the folds and achieving precise results.

Materials Needed: All you need to start is some origami paper or any square sheets of paper. Special origami paper often comes in vibrant colors and patterns, but standard paper can work as well.

Benefits and Enjoyment: Origami can be a meditative practice that improves dexterity and concentration. It's a rewarding hobby that offers endless possibilities for creating beautiful, handmade objects. Plus, completed pieces make unique gifts or decorative items for your home.

Start Drawing

Begin with Basics: Start by learning fundamental techniques such as sketching shapes, shading, and understanding perspective. You don't need to be an artist to begin; simple exercises will build your skills and confidence.

Gather Supplies: Invest in basic drawing tools like pencils, erasers, sketchbooks, and possibly some colored pencils or pens. Quality materials aren't necessary at first; basic supplies will suffice.

Take a Class or Online Course: Enroll in a local art class or explore online tutorials and courses. Many resources are available for free or at a low cost, offering structured guidance from experienced artists.

Practice Regularly: Dedicate time each day or week to drawing. Experiment with different subjects and styles to discover what you enjoy most. Remember, improvement comes with consistent practice and patience.

Knitting Joy

Versatile Creations: Knitting offers endless possibilities, from cozy scarves and hats to intricate sweaters and blankets. Whether you're crafting a simple pattern or taking on a more challenging project, there's always something new to create.

Tools of the Trade: All you need to get started are knitting needles, yarn, and a few basic supplies like scissors and a tape measure. Beginners can start with straightforward patterns, while more advanced knitters can explore complex designs.

Relaxing and Rewarding: Knitting is a soothing activity that allows you to unwind while producing something beautiful. The repetitive motion of the needles can be meditative, helping to reduce stress and increase focus.

A Gift from the Heart: Handmade knitwear makes for thoughtful and personalized gifts. Friends and family will appreciate the time and effort you put into creating something unique just for them.

Woodworking Mastery

Create Functional and Decorative Items: Discover the joy of crafting wooden furniture, decorative pieces, or even small household items. Woodworking allows you to create something tangible and useful, adding both beauty and functionality to your living space.

Learn the Craft: Start by taking a class at a local community center or online. Books and tutorials can also guide you through the basics, from understanding types of wood to mastering essential techniques.

Gather Essential Tools: Begin with a few basic tools like a saw, hammer, and chisel. As you progress, you can invest in more specialized equipment, such as a lathe for turning wood or a router for shaping edges.

Safety First: Always prioritize safety by wearing protective gear and learning how to use each tool properly. This ensures not only your well-being but also the quality of your work.

Pottery Craft

Creative Expression: Pottery offers a unique way to express creativity by shaping clay into various forms. You can create anything from simple bowls and mugs to intricate sculptures and decorative pieces.

Learning the Art: Start by taking local pottery classes or online tutorials. Many community centers and art studios offer beginner courses where you can learn the basics, such as hand-building techniques and wheel throwing.

Materials and Tools: To begin, you'll need clay, a pottery wheel (optional for hand-building), basic tools like carving knives and sponges, and access to a kiln for firing your creations. Some studios provide access to these tools for a fee.

Therapeutic Benefits: Engaging in pottery can be a calming and meditative experience. The tactile nature of working with clay helps reduce stress and improve focus, making it both a rewarding and relaxing hobby.

Crafting Models

Engaging Hobby: Building ship or airplane models offers a rewarding and immersive experience. It combines creativity with precision, allowing enthusiasts to delve into historical details and engineering marvels.

Getting Started: Begin with a basic kit that includes instructions and necessary materials. As skills progress, consider more complex models or even designing custom creations. Online forums and local clubs can provide valuable tips and support.

Materials and Tools: Essential tools include precision cutting tools, glue, paint, and fine brushes. Most model kits come with all necessary parts, but additional tools and materials may enhance the building experience and final result.

Benefits: This hobby promotes focus, patience, and hand-eye coordination. It can be a solitary activity or a social one if joining model-building groups.

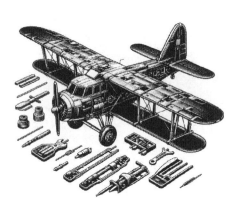

Custom Scents

Understand the Basics: Begin by learning about the different scent categories - top, middle, and base notes. Top notes are the initial, lighter scents; middle notes form the heart of the fragrance, and base notes provide depth and longevity.

Gather Your Supplies: You'll need essential oils, carrier oils (like jojoba or almond oil), alcohol (such as vodka), and small glass bottles for blending and storage. A pipette or dropper will help with precise measurements.

Experiment and Blend: Start with small test batches. Blend different essential oils to create a balanced fragrance. Keep track of your formulas, noting the number of drops used for each oil. This will help you refine your scent over time.

Test and Adjust: Let your perfume blend sit for a few days to allow the scents to meld. Test it on your skin and adjust the formula as needed. Patience is key, as scents evolve over time.

Classic Car Restoration

A Timeless Hobby: Restoring classic cars is a rewarding and engaging hobby that combines craftsmanship with a passion for automotive history. It offers a unique way to connect with the past while creating a beautiful, functional work of art.

Essential Tools and Skills: Successful restoration requires a variety of tools, from basic hand tools to specialized equipment. Key skills include mechanical knowledge, bodywork, and painting. There are numerous resources and communities available for learning and sharing expertise.

Project Satisfaction: The process of bringing a vintage vehicle back to life can be deeply satisfying. From sourcing rare parts to overcoming restoration challenges, each step is a triumph that culminates in a vehicle that tells its own story.

Community and Events: Engaging in classic car restoration opens up opportunities to join enthusiast clubs and attend car shows. These events provide a platform for showcasing your work, networking with fellow enthusiasts, and enjoying the camaraderie of shared interests.

Calligraphy Art

Understanding Calligraphy: Calligraphy is the art of beautiful writing. It blends form and function, using tools like pens and brushes to create visually appealing text. This practice emphasizes precision and creativity.

Exploring Styles: There are various calligraphy styles, from classic scripts like Italic and Gothic to modern forms. Each style offers unique techniques and historical background.

Creative Projects: Apply calligraphy to personalized stationery, invitations, artwork, and home décor. It transforms ordinary items into unique, meaningful creations.

Benefits and Learning: Calligraphy enhances fine motor skills and provides a relaxing, meditative experience. Learn through online courses, workshops, or self-study with books and practice sheets, making it a rewarding hobby.

Herbal Remedies

Discover the Power of Nature: Creating herbal remedies allows you to harness the healing properties of plants, providing a natural and effective way to support your health.

Health Benefits: Herbal medicines can boost immunity, reduce inflammation, and promote overall well-being. They offer a natural alternative to over-the-counter medications, often with fewer side effects.

Getting Started: Begin by researching common medicinal herbs like chamomile, peppermint, and lavender. Learn about their benefits, and consider starting a small herb garden or sourcing high-quality dried herbs.

Creative and Fulfilling: The process of making your own herbal remedies, such as teas, tinctures, and salves, can be both creative and rewarding. It offers a hands-on approach to wellness, connecting you with ancient traditions and nature's wisdom.

Reviving Old Furniture

Why It's Fascinating: Restoring old furniture breathes new life into cherished pieces, blending history with creativity. Each item carries a story, and the process of restoration allows you to preserve its legacy while adding your personal touch.

Getting Started: Begin by assessing the condition of the furniture. Clean it thoroughly and decide if it needs structural repairs, refinishing, or reupholstering. Research techniques that suit your skill level, whether it's simple repainting or advanced woodwork.

What You Need: Start with basic tools like sandpaper, paintbrushes, and varnish. Depending on the project, you might also need wood filler, screws, and upholstery materials. Having a dedicated workspace will help you stay organized.

The Reward: Restoring furniture is a fulfilling hobby that combines hands-on work with creative expression. The final result is a beautifully revived piece that can become a unique addition to your home or a thoughtful gift for someone special.

Crafting Soap or Candles

Start at Home: Making your own soap or candles is a creative and fulfilling hobby that can be done right from the comfort of your home. It requires minimal space and can be tailored to your preferences, from scents to colors.

Gather Supplies: For soap, you'll need a base like glycerin or lye, essential oils for fragrance, and molds to shape your creations. For candles, gather wax, wicks, fragrance oils, and molds or containers.

Learn the Basics: Begin with simple recipes and follow step-by-step instructions. Online tutorials, books, or local workshops can provide guidance on the techniques and safety precautions needed for both soap and candle making.

Experiment and Enjoy: As you gain confidence, experiment with different ingredients, shapes, and scents. This hobby not only allows you to create personalized products for yourself but also offers the opportunity to gift handmade items to friends and family.

Moments in Focus

Simple and Engaging: Photography is a fun and accessible hobby that anyone can start with little to no prior experience. It allows for creative expression and helps you see the world from different perspectives.

Choosing the Right Camera: For beginners, a compact digital camera or a smartphone with a good camera can be sufficient. As you grow more interested, consider investing in a DSLR or mirrorless camera to explore advanced features and enhance your skills.

Endless Possibilities: Photography offers numerous avenues to explore, from nature and portrait photography to urban and abstract styles. You can capture cherished moments, document travels, or experiment with artistic techniques.

Social and Learning Opportunities: Joining photography clubs, participating in workshops, or sharing your work online can connect you with like-minded individuals. It's a great way to learn, get feedback, and stay motivated.

Home Winemaking

Choose Your Ingredients: Begin with high-quality grapes or other fruits. Fresh, ripe fruit will produce the best results. You'll also need some basic equipment like a fermenter, a wine press, and bottles.

Understand the Process:
Winemaking involves several steps including crushing the fruit, fermenting the juice, and aging the wine. It's a relatively simple process once you familiarize yourself with the key stages.

Start Small: Begin with a small batch to practice and refine your technique. This allows you to experiment without committing to a large quantity and helps you learn the nuances of winemaking.

Follow Recipes and Guidelines:
Use trusted recipes or guides to ensure you're following best practices. Pay attention to measurements, fermentation times, and sanitation to avoid common pitfalls and achieve the best flavor.

Stained Glass Art

Introduction to Stained Glass: Stained glass involves arranging pieces of colored glass into patterns and securing them with lead or copper foil. This technique has been used for centuries to create beautiful windows, lamps, and decorative panels.

Getting Started: Choose a simple design to start with, such as a geometric pattern or a small panel. Trace your design onto a sheet of glass and cut the pieces according to the pattern. Once cut, fit the pieces together and use copper foil or lead came to join them.

Essential Tools and Materials: To begin, you'll need basic tools like glass cutters, pliers, a soldering iron, and a work surface. Additionally, you'll need sheets of stained glass, a pattern or design, and soldering supplies.

Finishing Touches: After assembling your design, use solder to secure the pieces and add any final details. Clean the glass and polish it to enhance its clarity and shine.

Chess Mastery

Engage Your Mind: Chess is a captivating game that challenges your intellect and strategic thinking. It's a mental workout that sharpens problem-solving skills and enhances memory, making it an excellent pastime for those looking to keep their minds active.

Develop Key Skills: Playing chess improves critical thinking, patience, and foresight. It teaches you to think several steps ahead, evaluate consequences, and make informed decisions - skills that are valuable in many aspects of life.

Join Tournaments: Chess offers numerous opportunities to connect with others through local clubs and online platforms. Participating in tournaments, whether friendly or competitive, can add an exciting dimension to your chess experience and allow you to meet like-minded individuals.

Lifelong Learning: Chess is a game of endless possibilities, with countless strategies to explore and master. Whether you're a beginner or an experienced player, there's always something new to learn, ensuring that the game remains engaging and fulfilling for years to come.

The Art of Collecting

A Timeless Hobby: Collecting is more than just acquiring items; it's a journey into the past, present, and future. It offers the joy of discovery, the thrill of the hunt, and the satisfaction of building something unique and personal.

What to Collect: The possibilities are endless - coins, stamps, vintage postcards, antiques, rare books, or even modern memorabilia like action figures or vinyl records. Your collection can reflect your passions and interests, making it a true reflection of who you are.

Exploring Auctions: Auctions, whether online or in-person, are fantastic places to find rare and valuable items. They also offer the excitement of bidding and winning that special piece you've been searching for. Learning the ins and outs of auctions can enhance your collecting experience.

Connecting with Fellow Collectors: Engaging with a community of collectors, whether through clubs, forums, or social media groups, can enrich your hobby. Sharing knowledge, trading items, and participating in events can make collecting a more rewarding and social experience.

Book Swap

For Avid Readers: A book swap with friends is a perfect way to indulge your love for reading. Sharing your favorite books allows you to introduce others to stories and ideas that have inspired you, while discovering new literary treasures through their recommendations.

Save Money: Regularly swapping books helps you save on the cost of buying new ones. Instead of purchasing, simply exchange what you've already read for something fresh, keeping your bookshelf dynamic without spending extra money.

Build Connections: Engaging in a book swap fosters deeper connections with friends. It provides opportunities for meaningful discussions and bonding over shared or differing opinions on the books exchanged.

Variety in Reading: Swapping books ensures a constant variety in your reading material. You might come across genres or authors you wouldn't normally choose, broadening your literary horizons and keeping your reading experience exciting.

Treasure Hunt

Explore Historical Sites: Start by selecting locations with rich histories, such as old battlefields, abandoned settlements, or ancient paths. These places are often treasure troves of forgotten artifacts waiting to be discovered.

Find Hidden Relics: With a metal detector, you can unearth a variety of items, from old coins and jewelry to long-lost tools and relics. Each find carries a story from the past, making the experience both exciting and educational.

Be Prepared: Equip yourself with the right tools, including a reliable metal detector, digging tools, and gloves. Research the area you plan to explore, and make sure you're aware of any local regulations regarding metal detecting.

Respect the Land: Always obtain permission before searching on private property and leave the area as you found it. The thrill of discovery is enhanced when you know you're preserving history for future generations to appreciate.

Travel and Adventure

RV Adventures

Ultimate Flexibility: An RV rental allows you to explore diverse destinations at your own pace. No need for fixed schedules or hotel reservations - just choose your route and enjoy the journey.

Choosing Your Route: Plan your route based on interests and preferences. Whether it's scenic routes through national parks, coastal drives, or a cross-country adventure, an RV lets you design your ideal travel experience.

Essential Packing: Pack wisely for comfort and convenience. Include clothing for various weather conditions, kitchen essentials, and personal items. Don't forget to bring along travel guides or maps to enhance your exploration.

Benefits of RV Travel: Enjoy the comfort of home on the road with amenities like a bed, bathroom, and kitchen. This mode of travel provides a unique way to connect with nature while maintaining the conveniences of home.

Rio's Samba Celebration

What It Is: The samba carnival is a dazzling celebration of Brazilian culture, known for its elaborate costumes, samba dance performances, and grand parades. It's a high-energy event where samba schools compete in a series of spectacular performances, showcasing their creativity and skill.

Why You Should Go: This carnival offers a unique opportunity to immerse yourself in a lively cultural tradition. The infectious rhythm of samba and the visual splendor of the parades create an unforgettable experience. It's also a chance to connect with people from around the world who share an appreciation for dance and music.

When and Where: The most famous samba carnival takes place in Rio de Janeiro, Brazil, usually during February or March, marking the beginning of Lent. It lasts for about a week, with the main parades occurring over the weekend.

What to Expect: Expect a vibrant atmosphere filled with music, dance, and celebration. The parades feature intricately designed floats and costumes, and the streets come alive with the rhythm of samba. Prepare for a sensory overload, with sights and sounds that will leave you with lasting memories.

Pedal Journeys

Unique Exploration: Cycling allows for a more intimate experience of your destination. You can access hidden spots and enjoy scenic routes that might be missed when traveling by car or train. It's a great way to immerse yourself in the local culture and landscape.

Health Benefits: This activity provides excellent cardiovascular exercise while allowing you to enjoy the outdoors. It can be adapted to various fitness levels, making it suitable for most people who are reasonably active.

Planning Your Route: Choose a route based on your interests and fitness level. Research cycling trails and maps to find paths that offer interesting sights and manageable distances. Consider starting with shorter trips to build endurance before tackling longer journeys.

Practical Considerations: Ensure your bike is in good condition and pack essential supplies such as repair kits, snacks, and weather-appropriate clothing. Accommodations should be planned ahead, especially if you're traveling through remote areas.

Machu Picchu Trail

Historic Path: The Inca Trail is a renowned trek leading to the ancient city of Machu Picchu in Peru. This trail has been used for centuries, offering a historical journey through stunning landscapes.

Scenic Beauty: The trail spans approximately 26 miles (42 kilometers) and winds through diverse terrains, including high-altitude mountain passes, lush cloud forests, and alpine tundra. Hikers are treated to breathtaking views of the Andes and ancient ruins.

Cultural Significance: Along the route, trekkers encounter archaeological sites such as the ruins of Wiñay Wayna and Sayacmarca. These remnants offer a glimpse into the Inca civilization and its remarkable engineering skills.

Preparation and Experience: The trek usually takes 4 days and requires a permit, which is limited and needs to be booked well in advance. The journey is challenging but rewarding, culminating in a grand arrival at Machu Picchu, one of the New Seven Wonders of the World.

Hitchhiking Wonders

Choosing Destinations: Opt for regions with a well-established hitchhiking culture or areas known for friendly locals. Smaller towns and rural areas often provide more opportunities for hitchhiking compared to busy urban centers.

Safety First: Always prioritize safety by informing someone you trust about your travel plans. Use a reliable map or GPS to track your route, and trust your instincts when accepting rides. Avoid hitchhiking at night or in isolated areas.

Packing Essentials: Bring only the essentials – a small backpack with water, snacks, a first-aid kit, and appropriate clothing for the weather. A sign with your destination can help drivers understand where you're headed.

Making Connections: Engage with drivers and fellow travelers to enrich your experience. Be respectful and friendly, as good communication can lead to unexpected opportunities and local insights.

Virtual Exploration

Expand Your Horizons: Virtual travel allows you to explore the world from the comfort of your home. With just a few clicks, you can visit famous landmarks, stroll through art museums, or even dive into the depths of the ocean - all without leaving your chair.

Global Adventures: Experience diverse cultures and environments as you virtually travel to countries you've always dreamed of visiting. Whether it's a tour of the pyramids in Egypt or a walk through the streets of Paris, virtual exploration brings the world to your fingertips.

How to Begin: Start your virtual journey by accessing various online platforms that offer guided tours, interactive maps, and 360-degree videos. Many museums, national parks, and tourist attractions provide free virtual tours that are both educational and entertaining.

Stay Curious: Virtual travel is an opportunity to continuously learn and discover. Whether you're interested in history, art, nature, or cuisine, there's always something new to explore. Embrace the possibilities and let your curiosity guide you to new and exciting experiences.

Private Vatican Tours

Exclusive Access: Enjoy the luxury of skipping long lines and exploring the Vatican Museums with a knowledgeable guide. Private tours often include early morning or after-hours access, allowing you to experience the art and history with fewer crowds.

Personalized Experience: Tailor your tour to your interests, whether it's Renaissance art, ancient sculptures, or the Vatican's rich history. Guides can focus on specific areas such as the Sistine Chapel, the Raphael Rooms, or the Vatican Library, based on your preferences.

In-Depth Knowledge: Benefit from the expertise of a private guide who provides detailed insights and fascinating stories behind the artworks and artifacts. Their deep knowledge enhances your understanding and appreciation of the museum's treasures.

Memorable Highlights: Marvel at Michelangelo's breathtaking frescoes in the Sistine Chapel, admire the grandeur of St. Peter's Basilica, and explore the vast collection of classical and Renaissance art. The intimate setting of a private tour allows for a deeper connection with these masterpieces.

Quad Fun

Choosing a Destination: Look for places known for quad biking, such as off-road parks, trails, or dedicated ATV (All-Terrain Vehicle) tracks. Popular spots often offer guided tours and well-maintained trails suitable for various skill levels.

Finding the Right Trail: Research local trails to match your skill level and interests. Some trails are designed for beginners with smoother paths, while others offer more challenging terrains for experienced riders. Websites and forums dedicated to ATV enthusiasts can be great resources.

Safety First: Ensure you have the proper safety gear, including a helmet, gloves, and protective clothing. It's also crucial to familiarize yourself with the safety guidelines and rules of the area where you'll be riding.

Renting or Buying: If you're new to quad biking, consider renting an ATV to start. Many rental companies provide all necessary equipment and offer guidance on how to operate the vehicle. If you're planning frequent rides, investing in your own ATV might be worth considering.

Kilimanjaro Ascent

Overview: Standing at 5,895 meters (19,341 feet), Kilimanjaro is a free-standing volcanic mountain located in Tanzania. It features three main peaks: Kibo, Mawenzi, and Shira. The climb offers a range of environments, from lush rainforests to stark alpine deserts.

Climbing Routes: There are several routes to the summit, such as Marangu, Machame, and Lemosho. Each route offers different experiences in terms of scenery and difficulty. The Machame route is known for its beautiful views, while the Lemosho route provides a more gradual ascent.

Preparation: Good physical fitness is essential for this trek. Focus on cardiovascular training and hiking to build endurance. It's wise to consult a medical professional to ensure you're fit for high-altitude trekking.

Practical Tips: To avoid altitude sickness, proper acclimatization is crucial. Ensure you have suitable gear for varying weather conditions and stay well-hydrated. Hiring a licensed guide is essential for safety and local knowledge.

Local Festivals & Celebrations

Types of Festivals: Look for food, music, cultural, or seasonal festivals in your area. These events often showcase local talents, crafts, and cuisines, providing a unique opportunity to learn more about your community's heritage.

Stay Informed: Keep an eye on community boards, social media, or local newspapers to find out about upcoming events. Websites and apps dedicated to local events can also provide information on dates, locations, and activities.

What to Bring: Pack essentials such as comfortable clothing and footwear, sunscreen, and a reusable water bottle. If you're attending a food festival, consider bringing cash for vendors who may not accept cards.

Engage with Others: Festivals are a great opportunity to meet new people and connect with neighbors. Participate in activities, try out new foods, or volunteer to help at a booth. Engaging with others can enhance your experience and create lasting memories.

Wonders of Egypt

Ancient Marvels: The Pyramids of Egypt, particularly the Great Pyramid of Giza, stand as one of the most remarkable architectural feats in human history. Built over 4,500 years ago, these structures continue to inspire awe and wonder.

Cultural Significance: The pyramids were originally constructed as tombs for pharaohs and are a testament to the ancient Egyptians' beliefs in the afterlife. Visiting these sites provides a deep connection to the rich cultural and spiritual traditions of the past.

Architectural Genius: The precision and skill involved in constructing the pyramids with limited technology remain a mystery. The alignment of the pyramids with celestial bodies showcases the ancient Egyptians' advanced understanding of astronomy and engineering.

A Timeless Experience: Standing before these colossal structures offers a unique sense of perspective and a chance to connect with history in a way that few other experiences can provide. A visit to the pyramids is not just a journey through space, but through time itself.

Cross-Country Trek

Choose Your Destination: Decide on a city or town you'd like to reach by foot. Consider the distance, the terrain, and the overall challenge it presents. Whether it's a nearby village or a destination across the country, the journey should be both exciting and achievable.

Plan Your Route: Research and map out the best route to take. Look for scenic paths, trails, and safe roads that offer a mix of natural beauty and convenience. Planning the route carefully ensures you can enjoy the journey while staying on track.

Prepare Physically: Walking long distances requires stamina and strength. Start a training regimen that includes daily walks, strength exercises, and stretching. Gradually increase your distance and intensity to build up your endurance for the trek.

Gather Essential Gear: Invest in good walking shoes, a comfortable backpack, and weather-appropriate clothing. Pack essentials like water, snacks, a first aid kit, and a map. Being well-prepared will make your journey more enjoyable and safe.

Battlefield Exploration

Step into History: Visiting historical battlefields offers a unique opportunity to immerse yourself in the past. Walking through these sites, you can imagine the soldiers who once stood on the same ground, bringing history to life in a way that books and documentaries can't.

Feel the Weight of Great Battles: Standing on a battlefield allows you to feel the significance of the events that took place there. The landscape, monuments, and preserved artifacts help you grasp the scale and impact of the battles that shaped history.

Expand Your Knowledge: Guided tours and interpretive centers often accompany these sites, providing detailed insights into the strategies, leaders, and outcomes of the battles. This enriches your understanding of the past and its relevance to the present.

Reflect on the Human Experience: Visiting these fields is not only about learning but also about reflection. You can contemplate the courage, sacrifice, and resilience of those who fought, gaining a deeper appreciation for the complexities of human history.

Way of St. James

Historical Importance: This ancient route has been traveled for over a thousand years by pilgrims seeking spiritual fulfillment. It culminates at the Cathedral of Santiago de Compostela, which is believed to house the remains of St. James, one of Jesus' apostles.

Diverse Landscapes: The Camino stretches approximately 500 miles (about 800 kilometers) from the French border to Santiago de Compostela. Along the way, walkers experience breathtaking views of mountains, rolling hills, and picturesque villages, each with its own unique charm.

Cultural Richness: The journey passes through various regions of Spain, including the Basque Country, Navarra, and Galicia. Each area offers a rich tapestry of history, architecture, and local cuisine, allowing travelers to immerse themselves in the culture.

Personal Reflection: Many people embark on this pilgrimage for personal reasons, finding it an opportunity for reflection and self-discovery. The trail fosters a sense of community among pilgrims, encouraging shared experiences and friendships along the way.

National Park Marvels

Breathtaking Scenery: National parks boast stunning landscapes, from majestic mountains and serene lakes to lush forests and expansive deserts. Each park has its own distinctive features, providing endless opportunities for awe and inspiration.

Wildlife Encounters: Observing wildlife in their natural habitats is a thrilling experience. National parks are home to diverse species, including rare and endangered animals. Spotting these creatures in the wild adds a special touch to any visit.

Outdoor Activities: Enjoy a range of activities tailored to different interests and abilities. Whether it's hiking, birdwatching, or simply enjoying a scenic drive, national parks offer something for everyone, encouraging both relaxation and adventure.

Educational Opportunities: Many parks provide educational programs and visitor centers where you can learn about the local ecosystems, geology, and history. Engaging with these resources enriches your visit and deepens your appreciation of nature.

World Cup Experience

Rare Opportunity: Attending the World Cup is a unique experience that happens only once every four years. It brings together teams from around the globe, creating a festive atmosphere and uniting fans in a shared passion for football.

Electric Atmosphere: The energy at the World Cup is unparalleled. From the moment you enter the stadium, the excitement is palpable. Fans from diverse backgrounds come together, cheering for their teams, creating a vibrant and electrifying environment.

Cultural Exchange: Visiting a host country for the World Cup offers a chance to experience its culture firsthand. Enjoy local cuisine, explore historical landmarks, and engage with fellow fans. It's an excellent way to immerse yourself in a different culture while celebrating the sport.

Memorable Connections: Sharing this experience with friends, family, or fellow football enthusiasts can forge lasting memories. The camaraderie built during matches, as well as the stories exchanged during travels, enhance the overall experience and create bonds that last a lifetime.

Grand Canyon Visit

Stunning Landscapes: The Grand Canyon's vast, colorful rock formations and unique geological layers provide a visual feast. From sunrise to sunset, the changing light dramatically alters the landscape, making each moment unique.

Vast Exploration: The Grand Canyon features a network of trails and scenic viewpoints that cater to all levels of fitness. Whether you prefer a leisurely walk along the rim or an adventurous descent into the canyon, there's a range of experiences to suit different interests and abilities.

Rich History: The canyon is not only a geological marvel but also a place with deep cultural significance. It has been a sacred site for Native American tribes for centuries and offers numerous opportunities to learn about their history and traditions.

Unique Wildlife: The diverse habitats within the canyon support a wide range of wildlife. Keep an eye out for mule deer, bighorn sheep, and a variety of bird species, all of which add to the richness of the visit.

Physical Activities

Dance Newness

Physical Benefits: Learning a new dance style is a great way to stay active and improve your physical health. Dance enhances cardiovascular fitness, flexibility, and strength while also being a fun way to exercise.

Mental Stimulation: Dance requires focus and memory, which can help keep your mind sharp. The challenge of learning new steps and routines stimulates cognitive function and can boost overall mental well-being.

Social Interaction: Taking dance classes or joining a dance group provides a chance to meet new people and engage in social activities. This can lead to new friendships and a sense of community, which is vital for maintaining a fulfilling social life.

Starting Out: Begin by choosing a dance style that interests you - whether it's salsa, ballroom, or contemporary. Look for local classes or online tutorials to get started. Embrace the learning process and have fun with it. Remember, it's never too late to start dancing and enjoy its many rewards.

Golfing Fun

Engaging Challenge: Golf is a game that combines skill, strategy, and precision. It provides a mental challenge that can be both stimulating and rewarding as you refine your technique and compete against yourself and others.

Great Exercise: Walking the course and swinging the club offers excellent low-impact exercise. This activity can help improve your cardiovascular health, flexibility, and overall physical fitness.

Social Interaction: Golf is a social sport that allows for meaningful interactions with others. Whether you're playing a round with friends, joining a local club, or participating in charity tournaments, golf creates opportunities for socializing and building new relationships.

Scenic Enjoyment: Golf courses are often situated in beautiful, tranquil environments. Spending time outdoors on a well-maintained course allows you to enjoy nature and fresh air while engaging in a pleasant activity.

Leap of Thrill

Unforgettable Thrills: Bungee jumping offers an exhilarating rush like no other. The moment you leap off the platform, you'll experience a unique blend of adrenaline and freedom, making for an unforgettable adventure.

Physical Readiness: While bungee jumping is accessible to many, it's important to be in good health. Ensure you're physically fit and clear of any medical conditions that could be exacerbated by the jump.

Safety First. Reputable bungee jumping operators prioritize safety. They use high-quality equipment and follow strict protocols. Always choose a provider with excellent reviews and safety records to ensure a secure experience.

Prepare for the Jump: Before you leap, take time to understand the process and listen to your instructor. Proper preparation and following guidelines will enhance your experience and ensure your safety.

Marathon Challenge

The History of the Marathon: The marathon traces its origins to ancient Greece, inspired by the legendary run of Pheidippides, who ran from the battlefield of Marathon to Athens to announce victory. This historic event evolved into the modern marathon race, first introduced in the 1896 Athens Olympics.

Race Distance: A standard marathon covers 26.2 miles (42.195 kilometers), a distance that challenges even the most seasoned athletes. It's a journey of endurance, where every mile tests your stamina and resolve.

Physical Preparation: Training for a marathon requires a well-structured plan that includes long runs, speed work, and strength training. It's crucial to build endurance gradually and maintain a balanced diet to support your body through the training process.

Mental Resilience: Completing a marathon is as much a mental challenge as it is physical. Developing mental toughness through visualization, goal setting, and staying motivated during tough training sessions is key to crossing the finish line.

Yoga Practice

Essence of Yoga: Yoga is a practice that integrates body, mind, and spirit through various postures, breathing exercises, and meditation techniques. Its origins trace back to ancient India, where it was developed to achieve balance and harmony.

Health Benefits: Engaging in yoga can enhance flexibility, strength, and balance. It promotes better posture, reduces stress, and can alleviate symptoms of anxiety and depression. Regular practice supports overall physical health and mental clarity.

Breathing Techniques: Pranayama, or controlled breathing, is a central component of yoga. Proper breathing techniques help in increasing lung capacity, improving oxygen flow to the brain, and calming the nervous system, which contributes to a sense of inner peace.

Mental and Emotional Well-being: Yoga encourages mindfulness and self-awareness. It helps in managing emotions, improving focus, and fostering a deeper connection with oneself. By incorporating meditation and relaxation, yoga can lead to a more centered and tranquil state of mind.

Skydiving Thrill

The Rush of Freefall: The sensation of freefall is both intense and liberating. As you jump from the plane, you'll experience a rush of adrenaline and a sense of weightlessness. The initial seconds of freefall are filled with excitement as you accelerate towards the ground before the parachute opens.

Physical Fitness: While skydiving does not require extreme physical fitness, a basic level of health and mobility is important. You should be able to comfortably sit and move during the jump and landing. It's advisable to consult with a doctor if you have any health concerns.

Safety Measures: Safety is a top priority in skydiving. Modern skydiving schools use state-of-the-art equipment and rigorous training to ensure a safe experience. Tandem jumps, where you're strapped to an experienced instructor, are ideal for beginners.

Preparation and Training: Before jumping, you'll undergo a comprehensive training session. This includes instructions on how to exit the plane, body position during freefall, and landing procedures. The training helps you understand the process and feel confident during the jump.

Equestrian Escape

Emotional Renewal: Interacting with horses provides a unique emotional uplift. Their gentle nature and intuitive responses help reduce stress and anxiety, offering a soothing break from city life. The calm and acceptance horses bring can be deeply therapeutic, promoting emotional balance.

Connection with Nature: Spending time with horses reconnects you with nature, offering a refreshing contrast to urban environments. The peaceful, natural settings where horses are kept contribute to relaxation and a sense of well-being.

Physical Benefits: Horseback riding and caring for horses provide physical exercise and improve coordination. The gentle movements of riding can enhance core strength and flexibility, benefiting overall physical health while providing a pleasurable activity.

Safety Considerations: Ensuring safety is key when starting horse riding. Choose reputable stables with experienced instructors. Wear proper gear, including helmets and boots, and start with basic lessons to build confidence and skill. Safety measures ensure a positive and secure experience.

Tai Chi Practice

Discover Balance and Harmony: Tai Chi, an ancient Chinese martial art, offers a gentle way to improve physical and mental well-being. Through slow, purposeful movements, it promotes balance, flexibility, and inner calm, making it an ideal practice for people of all ages.

Health Benefits: Regular Tai Chi practice can enhance cardiovascular health, reduce stress, and improve balance and coordination. It's especially beneficial for those looking to maintain mobility and a peaceful mind.

Getting Started: Begin your Tai Chi journey by finding a local class or online tutorials. Start with basic forms and focus on mastering the flow of movement. Even just a few minutes a day can bring noticeable improvements in your physical and mental state.

A Lifelong Practice: Tai Chi is not just exercise; it's a way of life. As you progress, you'll find that it offers endless opportunities for growth, both physically and mentally. The practice can be tailored to suit your individual needs and can be enjoyed solo or in a group setting, fostering a sense of community and shared purpose.

Stay Active

Health Benefits: Regular exercise at the gym helps improve cardiovascular health, strengthen muscles, and enhance flexibility. These physical benefits contribute to overall well-being and can help prevent various age-related ailments.

Mental Wellness: Engaging in gym workouts can also boost mental health. Exercise releases endorphins, reducing stress and anxiety while improving mood and cognitive function. It's a great way to keep both the body and mind sharp.

Social Interaction: Going to the gym offers an opportunity to meet new people and build friendships. Group classes or workout partners can make exercising more enjoyable and provide motivation to stay consistent.

Personal Achievement: Setting and reaching fitness goals, whether it's lifting heavier weights, increasing endurance, or simply maintaining regular gym attendance, fosters a sense of accomplishment and boosts self-esteem.

Surf's Up

Feel the Thrill: Surfing provides an unmatched thrill as you ride the waves. The sensation of gliding on water and the challenge of balancing on a board create a sense of freedom and accomplishment that's hard to find elsewhere.

What You Need: Essential gear includes a surfboard suited to your skill level, a wetsuit (if surfing in colder waters), and a leash to keep the board attached to you. A good surf instructor or surf school can also help you get started.

Prepare for the Waves: Start by taking a few lessons to learn the basics, including paddling, popping up, and riding small waves. Understanding ocean safety and etiquette is crucial. Regular practice will help improve your technique and confidence.

Embrace the Journey: Surfing is as much about the experience as it is about the sport. Each session brings new challenges and triumphs, making it a rewarding pursuit that enriches both your physical and mental well-being.

Tennis Time

Effective Exercise: Playing tennis provides a full-body workout, enhancing cardiovascular health, strength, and flexibility. The fast-paced nature of the game helps to burn calories and improve overall fitness.

Easy to Start: Tennis is accessible to players of all skill levels. Beginners can quickly pick up the basics and start playing, while more experienced players can enjoy the challenge of refining their skills.

Social Interaction: Tennis is a social sport that allows you to meet new people and build friendships. Whether you join a local league or play with friends, it's a fun way to connect with others.

Mental Stimulation: The strategic elements of tennis keep your mind engaged. The game requires focus, quick thinking, and problem-solving, which can help keep your mind sharp and alert.

Dive Into the Deep

Explore Underwater Beauty: Diving offers an unparalleled opportunity to witness the stunning beauty of the underwater world. Colorful coral reefs, vibrant marine life, and breathtaking landscapes await beneath the surface, providing an immersive experience that connects you with nature.

Getting Started: To begin your diving journey, consider enrolling in a certified diving course from a reputable provider. These courses offer essential training, ensuring you understand safety protocols, equipment usage, and diving techniques.

Essential Equipment: Basic diving gear includes a wetsuit or drysuit, mask, snorkel, fins, and a buoyancy control device (BCD). Additionally, a regulator and a tank for air supply are crucial. Many dive shops offer rental equipment, making it easy to start without a significant initial investment.

Join a Community: Engaging with fellow diving enthusiasts can enhance your experience. Local dive clubs and online communities provide opportunities to share knowledge, find dive buddies, and discover new dive sites. Participating in group dives can also increase safety and enjoyment.

Style and Image Updates

Hair Makeover

Transform Your Style: Changing your hairstyle can refresh your overall appearance and boost your confidence. Whether you opt for a drastic change or a subtle update, this is an opportunity to express your personality in a new way.

Experiment with Length: For men, growing or shaving a beard or mustache can create a significant transformation. Women might consider switching up their hair length - growing it out for a softer look or cutting it short for something bold and edgy.

Explore New Textures and Colors: Add some flair by trying new hair textures, like curls or waves, or experimenting with different hair colors. A fresh color can completely alter your look, making you feel rejuvenated.

Seek Professional Advice: Consult with a hairstylist to find the best style that complements your face shape, lifestyle, and preferences. Sometimes, a slight tweak in your hairstyle can make a big difference.

Inked Milestones

Marking a New Chapter: A tattoo can symbolize a fresh start and the new phase of life. It offers a unique way to celebrate personal growth, new interests, or cherished memories. Choosing a design that resonates with you can make this transition more meaningful.

Design Choices: Consider designs that reflect your passions, achievements, or personal philosophy. Whether it's a symbol of a significant life event, a favorite quote, or artwork that speaks to you, the design should be something you'll cherish for years to come.

Temporary vs. Permanent: Decide if you want a permanent tattoo or a temporary one. Temporary tattoos are a great way to experiment with designs and placements without committing long-term. They can also be a fun way to explore different styles before making a permanent decision.

Consulting a Professional: When opting for a permanent tattoo, it's essential to consult with a skilled tattoo artist. They can help refine your design, ensure proper placement, and offer advice on aftercare to maintain the tattoo's quality over time.

Style Upgrade

Embrace Change: See this as an opportunity to reinvent yourself. Let go of outdated styles and explore new fashion trends that align with your current tastes and preferences. This can be both fun and empowering.

Declutter: Go through your existing clothes and assess what no longer fits or suits your new vision. Donate or recycle items that you no longer wear. This not only clears space but also helps others in need.

Experiment Boldly: Don't be afraid to step out of your comfort zone. Try new colors, patterns, and styles that you haven't considered before. This is your chance to express a new aspect of your personality through your clothing.

Invest in Versatility: Choose pieces that can be mixed and matched to create various looks. This ensures that your wardrobe remains fresh and adaptable, making it easier to keep your style updated.

Beauty Enhancements

Assess Your Motivations: Take time to reflect on why you're considering cosmetic surgery. Whether it's to boost confidence, address aging concerns, or enhance your appearance, understanding your motivations is essential for making informed decisions.

Consult a Specialist: Schedule consultations with board-certified plastic surgeons or dermatologists. They can provide professional advice tailored to your needs, helping you understand the procedures, expected outcomes, and potential risks involved.

Explore Options: Research various procedures available, from non-invasive treatments like Botox to more extensive surgeries like facelifts or body contouring. Each option has unique benefits, risks, and recovery times, so gathering information is crucial.

Consider the Aftermath: Think about the recovery process and how it may impact your daily life. Discuss post-operative care and any necessary lifestyle adjustments with your specialist to ensure a smooth transition.

New Nutrition Path

Health Benefits: Adopting a new eating plan can help manage or prevent chronic conditions such as diabetes, heart disease, and obesity. A balanced diet rich in fruits, vegetables, whole grains, and lean proteins can enhance overall health and vitality.

Explore New Options: Trying different diets, such as the Mediterranean, plant-based, or DASH diet, can provide variety and excitement in meals. Each of these diets emphasizes different food groups and can lead to improved health outcomes.

Listen to Your Body: It's essential to pay attention to how certain foods affect your body. Keeping a food diary can help identify which foods boost your energy and which may cause discomfort or allergies.

Consider Individual Needs: Age, lifestyle, and health conditions play a crucial role in determining dietary needs. Consulting with a healthcare professional or nutritionist can provide personalized recommendations tailored to your unique situation.

Digital World

Start a Blog or Vlog

Choosing Your Platform: Decide whether a written blog or a video blog (vlog) suits your style better. Platforms like WordPress, Blogger, or YouTube are popular and user-friendly options that allow you to easily set up and manage your content.

Finding Your Niche: Identify topics you are passionate about, whether it's travel, cooking, gardening, or technology. Focusing on a niche that excites you will make it easier to create content consistently and attract an audience interested in those subjects.

Creating Content: Start by planning your posts or videos. Outline your ideas and create a content calendar to keep yourself organized. Regular updates are key to maintaining and growing your audience, so try to post consistently, whether that's weekly, bi-weekly, or monthly.

Growing Your Audience: Share your blog or vlog on social media, engage with your followers, and interact with other content creators in your niche. As your blog or vlog grows, consider monetizing your content through ads, sponsored posts, or affiliate marketing to earn a little extra income.

Build Your Website

Define Your Purpose: Determine the primary goal of your website. Whether you want to showcase a portfolio, share a blog, or promote a small business, knowing your purpose will guide the design and content.

Choose a Platform: Select a website builder that suits your needs and technical skills. Platforms like WordPress, Wix, or Squarespace offer user-friendly options that don't require coding knowledge.

Content and Design: Organize your content logically, ensuring it's engaging and easy to navigate. Choose a design that reflects your style and purpose. Incorporate images, videos, and other media to make your site visually appealing.

Launch and Maintain: Once your site is built, publish it and share it with your network. Regularly update your content to keep it fresh and relevant. Consider adding new features or expanding your site as your needs evolve.

Podcasting Fun

Find Your Niche: Choose a topic you're passionate about and knowledgeable in. This could be anything from hobbies, travel, or personal experiences. Your enthusiasm will engage your audience and make your podcast stand out.

Plan Your Episodes: Outline your content and format. Decide on the frequency of episodes, the length of each podcast, and the structure (e.g., interviews, solo discussions). Having a clear plan will help maintain consistency and quality.

Set Up Your Equipment: Invest in a good-quality microphone and headphones. Platforms like Anchor, Podbean, and Libsyn can help you distribute your podcast to major directories such as Apple Podcasts, Spotify, and Google Podcasts. A quiet space for recording will also enhance sound quality.

Promote and Invite Guests: Share your podcast on social media, relevant forums, and with your network to attract listeners. Inviting guests with interesting perspectives can add variety and draw in their followers as well.

Building a Social Group

Community Building: A Facebook group helps connect individuals with similar interests, hobbies, or life stages. This creates a supportive community where members can share experiences, advice, and encouragement.

Local Solutions: It can address local issues or needs by facilitating discussions and organizing events within the group. Members can collaborate on solutions to common problems or plan local meet-ups.

Information Sharing: The group serves as a hub for exchanging useful information, such as local services, activities, and resources. It allows for easy access to relevant updates and announcements.

Enhanced Engagement: Engaging in a Facebook group promotes social interaction and keeps members actively involved. This can lead to new friendships, networking opportunities, and a sense of belonging.

Code & Create

Mental Stimulation: Learning programming stimulates the mind, enhancing cognitive abilities and problem-solving skills. It engages critical thinking and logical reasoning, which can keep the brain active and sharp.

Creative Outlet: Programming allows for creative expression through designing websites and developing smartphone apps. It offers a platform to build and bring unique ideas to life, turning concepts into functional projects.

Accessible Learning: Starting with programming is easier than ever. Numerous online resources, including tutorials and interactive courses, are available to guide beginners through the basics and beyond. Many platforms offer step-by-step instructions and community support.

Practical Applications: Knowledge of coding can lead to practical outcomes, such as creating personal websites, developing mobile apps, or even contributing to open-source projects. This skill can be both a fulfilling hobby and a useful tool for various digital needs.

Digital Currency Exploration

Understanding Modern Money: Cryptocurrency represents a new era of digital finance, with Bitcoin, Ethereum, and other coins leading the way. Learning about these currencies can provide insights into how they function and their impact on the global economy.

Sharing Knowledge: Understanding blockchain and cryptocurrencies can enrich your conversations, whether in blogs, podcasts, or discussions with friends. Sharing insights about digital currency can spark interesting dialogues and inform others about this evolving field.

Investing Wisely: As interest in cryptocurrencies grows, so does the potential for investment. However, it's crucial to approach this market cautiously. Research different coins, their technologies, and market trends before making any financial commitments.

Keeping Updated: The cryptocurrency landscape is continually changing. Following reputable sources, joining online communities, and participating in educational courses can help you stay informed about the latest developments and investment strategies.

Volunteering

Animal Shelters

Significance of the Role: Volunteering at an animal shelter provides essential support to the organization, helping to care for and find homes for animals in need. Your efforts directly contribute to improving the lives of these animals and support the shelter's mission.

Where to Help: Look for animal shelters or rescue organizations in your community. Many shelters have websites or social media pages where they post volunteer opportunities and contact information. Reach out to them to inquire about their needs and how you can assist.

What to Do: Volunteer tasks can range from feeding and grooming animals to cleaning kennels and assisting with adoption events. Some shelters may also offer opportunities for training in specific skills like animal behavior or administration.

Getting Started: To begin, contact your local shelter to learn about their volunteer requirements and orientation process. Many shelters provide training for new volunteers, ensuring you're prepared to contribute effectively and safely.

Political Volunteer

Make a Difference: By volunteering, you can contribute to shaping policies and electing leaders who align with your values. Your efforts help amplify the voices and causes you care about, influencing important decisions at local, regional, or national levels.

Learn and Grow: Engaging in a campaign provides valuable insights into the political process and grassroots organizing. You'll gain experience in public speaking, event planning, and strategic communication, enhancing your skills and knowledge in the political arena.

Connect with Others: Volunteering offers the chance to meet and collaborate with like-minded individuals who share your interests. Building a network of contacts in the political sphere can lead to new friendships and opportunities for collaboration on future projects.

Stay Active and Engaged: Participating in a campaign keeps you engaged with current events and community issues. It provides a sense of purpose and accomplishment, keeping you active and involved in meaningful activities that impact society.

Nature Guardians

Participate in Local Cleanups: Engage in or organize community clean-up events to remove trash from parks, beaches, and natural areas. This hands-on approach helps maintain the beauty and health of local ecosystems.

Support Conservation Projects: Volunteer with organizations dedicated to wildlife preservation and habitat restoration. Activities may include planting trees, monitoring wildlife populations, or assisting in habitat restoration efforts.

Educate and Advocate: Share knowledge about environmental issues and conservation efforts with others. Volunteer to lead educational programs in schools or community groups, advocating for sustainable practices and raising awareness about local environmental challenges.

Assist in Research and Monitoring: Get involved in scientific research by volunteering to help collect data, monitor species, or track environmental changes. Many organizations welcome volunteers to support their research and provide valuable assistance in data collection and analysis.

Giving Back

Diverse Opportunities: There are numerous ways to contribute, from helping out in local shelters, food banks, and community centers to assisting in hospitals or clinics. Tasks can range from administrative support and event organizing to direct patient care or mentoring.

Sense of Fulfillment: Engaging in volunteer work provides a profound sense of satisfaction. Knowing that your efforts make a difference in someone's life can be incredibly fulfilling and offers a unique sense of purpose.

Community Connection: Volunteering helps you connect with your community. It's a way to meet new people, build relationships, and strengthen social ties. This connection can enhance your feeling of belonging and make you an integral part of your local area.

Skill Utilization and Growth: You can apply your existing skills in a new context while also learning new ones. Volunteering allows you to use your expertise in meaningful ways, fostering personal growth and development.

Creative Expressions

Take the Stage

Embrace the Challenge: Stand-up comedy is an exhilarating way to step out of your comfort zone and hone your public speaking skills. It offers a platform to share your unique perspective with an audience, building confidence and communication abilities in a fun, engaging way.

Start Small: Begin by attending local comedy shows and open mic nights to get a feel for the environment. Observe different comedians, their timing, and delivery. You can even start practicing with friends or family to build your material and refine your style.

Write and Practice: Developing your set is key. Write jokes that resonate with your life experiences and personality. Practice delivering them aloud, focusing on timing, pacing, and audience interaction. The more you rehearse, the more comfortable you'll feel when it's time to perform.

Take the Leap: When you're ready, sign up for an open mic night or a local comedy club event. Remember, the goal is to have fun and express yourself. Whether your jokes land or not, the experience itself is rewarding, helping you grow as a communicator and entertainer.

Showtime

Discover the Variety: There are numerous types of TV shows that you can apply to participate in, from talent competitions and game shows to reality series and talk shows. Research which type resonates most with your interests and skills.

Find the Right Show: Look for shows that are actively seeking participants. This information is often available on the show's official website or social media platforms. Consider shows that align with your talents, hobbies, or unique life experiences.

Prepare Your Application: Each show has its own application process. Generally, you will need to fill out an application form, provide a video audition or introduction, and possibly attend an in-person casting call. Ensure you follow all guidelines and showcase your personality and enthusiasm.

Showcase Your Unique Qualities: Highlight what makes you stand out. Whether it's a special skill, a compelling story, or a unique perspective, make sure to convey what you bring to the table. Enthusiasm and authenticity are key to making a memorable impression.

Write a Book

Share Your Expertise: Writing a book allows you to share your professional knowledge and insights with others. Consider what valuable lessons or experiences you have that could benefit readers. Reflect on your unique perspective and how it can enrich your audience.

Crafting Your Manuscript: Begin by outlining your ideas and structuring your content into a logical flow. Write consistently and set manageable milestones to stay motivated. Seek feedback from colleagues or professional editors to enhance your manuscript's quality.

Publishing Choices: Explore different publishing options, including traditional, self-publishing, or hybrid models. Each has its advantages, so choose the one that aligns with your goals and resources. Understand the requirements and processes involved in each publishing route.

Marketing Your Book: Develop a marketing plan to promote your book effectively. Utilize social media, book launches, and networking opportunities to reach your target audience. Engaging with potential readers through blogs, interviews, or speaking events can also help increase your book's visibility.

Reporting for the Local Paper

Focus on Community Issues: Address local problems and concerns that matter to your neighbors. Whether it's about new developments, community services, or local events, highlighting these issues can foster greater community awareness and action.

Engage with Residents: Talk to people in your community to understand their perspectives and concerns. Gathering input from diverse voices ensures your articles reflect the true pulse of the neighborhood and provide valuable insights.

Provide Solutions: Alongside reporting issues, suggest possible solutions or ways the community can address them. Offering constructive ideas can inspire action and demonstrate a proactive approach.

Build Connections: Writing for a local paper helps build connections with fellow residents and local organizations. It's a way to become more involved and informed about your community while contributing to its growth and improvement.

Choral Harmony

Join Local Choirs: Many communities have local choirs or vocal groups that welcome new members. These groups range from amateur to semi-professional levels and often perform at local events or concerts. Check community centers, churches, or online platforms for information on available choirs.

Start a Group: If you can't find a choir that suits your interests, consider starting your own. Gather a few friends or acquaintances who enjoy singing, and meet regularly to practice and perform together. This can be a fun way to build camaraderie and share your love of music.

Explore Online Options: Online singing groups and virtual choirs have become increasingly popular. Platforms like Zoom or social media offer opportunities to join groups and participate in virtual rehearsals and performances, making it easy to connect with others from the comfort of your home.

Attend Workshops and Festivals: Look for local workshops, music festivals, or community events focused on vocal performance. These events can provide valuable opportunities to hone your skills, meet other singers, and enjoy the vibrant world of choral music.

Hodgepodge

Regular Health Checkups

Preventive Care: Regular medical checkups are crucial for detecting potential health issues before they become serious. Many conditions can develop silently, and early detection often leads to better treatment outcomes.

Age-Related Risks: As people age, the risk of chronic illnesses increases. Routine examinations help monitor vital signs, blood pressure, cholesterol levels, and other health markers that can indicate underlying problems.

Personalized Health Plans: Regular visits allow healthcare providers to create tailored health plans that address individual needs, including lifestyle adjustments, medications, and screenings. This personalized approach enhances overall well-being.

Maintaining Peace of Mind: Knowing your health status can reduce anxiety and promote a proactive approach to well-being. Regular checkups provide an opportunity to discuss any concerns with your healthcare provider and receive professional guidance.

Small Ventures

Leverage Your Expertise: Utilize your accumulated knowledge and skills to offer valuable services or advice. Your experience can provide unique insights and solutions that others may not have, giving you a competitive edge.

Sense of Purpose: Engaging in a business or consulting role can create a sense of purpose and accomplishment. Contributing to projects or helping clients solve problems can be highly rewarding and keep you motivated.

Financial Benefits: Starting a small business or offering consulting services can provide an additional source of income. With careful planning and execution, you can generate revenue while enjoying the flexibility of being your own boss.

Networking Opportunities: Launching a business or consulting practice opens up new networking opportunities. Building professional relationships can lead to new projects, partnerships, and personal growth.

Adopting a Companion

Emotional Joy: Bringing a pet into your life can fill your days with love and companionship. The bond formed with a furry friend can provide emotional support, reduce feelings of loneliness, and enhance overall well-being.

Choosing the Right Pet: When considering adoption, think about your lifestyle and preferences. Dogs, cats, rabbits, and even birds have unique personalities and needs. Take the time to research which type of pet aligns best with your living situation and activity level.

Rescue and Support: Adopting from a shelter means giving a homeless animal a second chance. Shelters often provide vaccinations and spaying/neutering, ensuring you start your journey on the right foot. Plus, you'll be supporting organizations that dedicate their resources to animal welfare.

Enriching Life: Owning a pet encourages physical activity, whether it's walking a dog or playing with a cat. Engaging with a pet can lead to new social opportunities, from meeting fellow pet owners to participating in community events, enriching your life in meaningful ways.

Plant a Tree

Contributing to Nature: By planting a tree, you help combat climate change, enhance local biodiversity, and improve air quality. Trees play a crucial role in sustaining our environment and providing habitat for wildlife.

Emotional Satisfaction: The act of planting a tree can be deeply fulfilling. It provides a sense of accomplishment and connection to the earth, fostering a lasting bond with the environment. Watching the tree grow over time can be a source of joy and pride.

Choosing the Right Tree: Select a tree species that is well-suited to your local climate and soil conditions. Native species are often the best choice as they support local wildlife and are adapted to the local environment. Consider factors such as tree size, growth rate, and maintenance needs when making your selection.

Educational Value: Planting a tree offers a chance to learn about different species and their ecological benefits. Sharing this knowledge with others can help raise awareness about environmental conservation and inspire similar actions.

Shark Diving

Thrill of a Lifetime: Shark diving offers an unparalleled thrill, immersing you in the heart of the ocean with some of its most majestic and formidable inhabitants. Whether with a cage for safety or in open water for the bravest souls, the experience is unforgettable.

Safety First: Most shark dives are conducted with the option of a protective cage, especially for those new to the sport. For more experienced divers, cage-free options are available, providing an exhilarating way to interact with these incredible creatures.

Planning Your Dive: To embark on a shark diving adventure, choose a reputable dive operator that adheres to strict safety and environmental standards. Popular locations include the Bahamas, South Africa, and Australia, where you can experience diverse shark species and dive conditions.

Memorable Experience: Beyond the adrenaline rush, shark diving offers profound encounters with nature. You'll gain a deeper understanding of these often-misunderstood animals and their role in marine ecosystems, making for a once-in-a-lifetime experience that will leave lasting memories.

Flea Market Finds

Unique Treasures: Flea markets are treasure troves of unique and eclectic items. From vintage clothing to rare collectibles, you can discover items that aren't found in regular stores. It's a chance to own something truly one-of-a-kind.

Historical Artifacts: Many flea markets feature historical items that offer a glimpse into the past. Whether it's antique furniture, old books, or retro gadgets, these artifacts carry stories and charm from bygone eras.

Bargain Hunting: Negotiating prices at flea markets is part of the fun. You can often find high-quality items at a fraction of their retail price. It's a great way to stretch your budget while enjoying the thrill of the hunt.

Local Crafts and Goods: Flea markets often showcase handmade crafts and local goods. Supporting artisans and small businesses not only provides you with unique items but also helps sustain local economies.

Flash Mob Fun

What It Is: A flash mob involves a group of individuals converging in a public space to engage in a coordinated activity, such as dancing, singing, or acting. These events are usually planned secretly and executed in a surprising, entertaining manner.

How They Manifest: Flash mobs are often organized through social media or messaging apps. Participants receive instructions about the time, place, and specific actions to perform. The element of surprise is key, creating a memorable experience for both participants and onlookers.

Where They Occur: These gatherings can take place in various public locations, such as parks, shopping malls, or public squares. The choice of location often aligns with the theme or purpose of the flash mob, ensuring it has a significant impact on the audience.

Getting Involved: To participate, look for local flash mob groups or events online. Join their networks to stay updated on upcoming activities. Following the instructions provided and arriving on time will ensure you are part of the fun and contribute to the success of the event.

Gratitude List

Reflect on Your Life: Take a moment to think about the people, experiences, and moments that have brought joy and fulfillment. Consider relationships with family and friends, personal achievements, and simple pleasures that have enriched your life.

Write Down Your Thoughts: Start jotting down everything you're grateful for, no matter how big or small. This could include meaningful connections, personal growth, or even everyday comforts like a warm cup of tea. Aim to be specific and detailed.

Organize Your List: Group similar items together or create categories, such as relationships, experiences, and accomplishments. This can help you see patterns and appreciate the various aspects of your life more fully.

Review and Reflect: Regularly revisit your list to remind yourself of the positive things in your life. This practice can boost your mood, enhance your outlook, and foster a sense of contentment.

Digital Detox Week

Enhanced Focus: Without constant notifications, you'll find it easier to concentrate on tasks and enjoy activities without distractions. This can lead to more productivity and a deeper engagement with hobbies or projects you've been putting off.

Improved Relationships: Being present in the moment allows for more meaningful interactions with family and friends. Face-to-face conversations become more rewarding, and you'll have the chance to truly connect without the interruption of a screen.

Reduced Stress: Constant exposure to digital media can contribute to stress and anxiety. Taking a break helps reduce information overload and gives your mind a chance to relax, leading to a calmer and more balanced state of being.

Self-Discovery: Without your smartphone as a constant companion, you may discover new interests and hobbies or rekindle old ones. This time can be used for self-reflection and personal growth, as you'll have the opportunity to engage in activities that genuinely interest you without digital distractions.

Message in a Bottle

Unique Experience: Sending a message in a bottle is a timeless and intriguing activity that combines creativity and adventure. It's an opportunity to craft a personal note or story that could one day be discovered by someone far away.

What to Write: Consider writing about your hopes, dreams, or a piece of advice. You could include a poem, a favorite quote, or even a small sketch. Make sure to date your message and include your contact information if you hope for a reply.

Choosing the Location: Pick a location with a strong current to increase the chances of your bottle traveling far. Popular spots include oceans, large rivers, or remote beaches. Research local laws to ensure it's legal and environmentally friendly.

The Launch: Seal your message in a waterproof bottle, perhaps with a small keepsake. Once you've selected the spot, cast your bottle into the water and let the currents take it on its journey. Whether it's found or not, you'll have created a unique connection with the wider world.

Year-Round Harvest

Fresh Produce Anytime: Building a greenhouse allows you to enjoy fresh vegetables and herbs throughout the year, regardless of the weather. This controlled environment extends your growing season, letting you cultivate a variety of plants even in colder months.

Sustainable Living: A greenhouse promotes self-sufficiency by reducing your reliance on store-bought produce. Growing your own food means fewer trips to the grocery store and a smaller carbon footprint.

Healthy Hobby: Gardening in a greenhouse is a rewarding activity that keeps you physically active and mentally engaged. It provides a peaceful space to connect with nature and enjoy the therapeutic benefits of nurturing plants.

Customizable Space: You can design your greenhouse to fit your needs, whether you're looking to grow a few herbs or maintain a full vegetable garden. From small kits to larger structures, greenhouses can be tailored to suit any space and gardening ambitions.

Home Museum

Select a Theme: Begin by choosing a theme that reflects your life experiences or passions. This could be anything from family heritage to a collection of travel souvenirs or cherished hobbies. Your chosen theme will guide what you gather and display.

Designate a Space: Dedicate a specific area in your home, whether a room, a corner, or a few shelves, for your collection. Arrange the items thoughtfully, creating a space that is both accessible and visually engaging.

Gather and Preserve: Collect meaningful items that align with your theme, such as photographs, letters, antiques, or memorabilia. Take care to preserve these items, using archival materials when needed to ensure their longevity.

Share Your Story: Invite friends and family to explore your home museum. Sharing the stories behind your collection adds a personal touch and allows you to connect with others while preserving your legacy.